The Rendezvous

Embracing beauty in life's many faces!

RENU PANDEY

Made with ❤ on the BookLeaf Publishing Platform
www.bookleafpub.in
www.bookleafpub.com

To the seekers of resilience and fortitude,

To the souls who find solace in words

To the countless hearts who have weathered storms,

and emerged stronger, braver and more compassionate

This book is a tribute to your journey.

To the ones who walk the path of life with truth, hope and an unwavering heart.

To the readers who seek meaning in the pages of this book,

who find comfort in stories and the power of poetry,

May you discover within these words

The courage to face your fears, the hope to chase your dreams

And the love to cherish each moment.

Let's bring some beauty to the world together.

Acknowledgement

Writing a book is not a solitary journey, and this collection of poems is no exception. There are many individuals who have played a crucial role in its creation, and I am deeply grateful for their support and encouragement.

First and foremost, I extend my heartfelt thanks to my family, friends and my students, whose unwavering belief in me and my work has been a constant source of inspiration. Your patience, understanding and encouragement have been the bedrock upon which this book stands.

A special thank you to my readers, whose enthusiasm and support have fuelled my passion for writing. Your feedback, kind words and shared experiences have given me the courage to continue exploring and expressing through poetry.

To the publishing team, your expertise and dedication have brought this book to life. I appreciate the time, effort and care you have invested in ensuring that these poems find their way to readers.

Finally, I am deeply thankful for the quiet moments of reflection and inspiration that have allowed me to explore the depths of my thoughts and emotions. It is in these moments that the essence of this collection was born.

To all who have been a part of this journey, your support has made this endeavour possible. I dedicate this book to you with sincere gratitude and appreciation.

With heartfelt thanks,
Renu Pandey

Preface

There are moments in life when the epiphany hits, and it serves as a powerful turning point where we start reflecting on the paths we've walked, the dreams we've chased, the struggles we have endured and the lessons we've learned. Poetry, for me, has always been a way to capture these fleeting moments—an attempt to understand the complexity of life and the simplicity of truth.

This collection of poems is a journey through a deeper realisation of myself. The myriad of emotions, experiences and revelations that have shaped my understanding of the world. Each poem is a reflection of a thought, a memory or a question that lingered in my mind, demanding to be explored and expressed.

As you turn these pages, I hope you find echoes of your own journey within these lines. Poetry has a unique way of connecting us—across time, space and experience—and my greatest wish is that they resonate with you, offering comfort, insight or simply a moment of reflection.

This book is not just a collection of poems; it is a conversation between us—a sharing of thoughts, feelings and observations that bind us together in our shared humanity. I invite you to read with an open heart, to linger on the words that speak to you and to find your own meaning in the spaces between the lines.

Thank you for embarking on this journey with me. May these poems inspire you to see the beauty in every day, the strength in vulnerability and the hope that lies within each of us.

With gratitude and warmth,
Renu Pandey

1. The Rendezvous with My Broken Self!

Rising from the ashes,

Soaring to the skies

With the twigs & tinders

Gathered in autumn

I weaved a beguiling nest

And called it mine!

You set it ablaze, mercilessly

A several times

Disguised under the smoke

There lies

Unwavering flames, refusing to die!

My wings are singed, my feathers are torn

Yet in my heart, new hope is born

With every dark, I find my way

Turning darkness into the brightest day!

You thought the flames would see me fall

But I have learned to rise above all

For in the ashes, life remains

And from the dust, I break my chains!

Beckoning you,

Is the crackling pyre in your eyes

Averting your gaze

The fidgeting I perceive

Your repentance I proclaim

For the rekindling within me

You had wanted to tame!

Another morning it is,

Covered with frost &dew

Nothing is the same,

The tides have turned

And the seasons are new!

The winds whisper of change

Of paths that once were true

Now, altered by time's gentle hand

And the world wears a different hue!

You covet it again

Like back then

When hearts were wild

And dreams were penned!

You reach for me with hands that yearn

For something lost, yet to burn!

Failing to realise

The fumes are for the skies

And aiming the highs

It's long lost, my dear!

Gone forever!!!

2. Your Time To Shine

When the incessant endeavours

All go awry!

And the lancinating pain

Asks you the reason why

When the dreams are high

And the hopes are dim!

When life seems cold and wind grows fierce

Let resilience be the sword you pierce

Through every storm, through every fight

Remember, dawn follows every night.

When serendipity situates no mercy
You crouch and plead
Until you bleed
But that's not what you need!

For in the shadows, strength resides
Beneath the weight of crashing tides
Each stumble is a step towards grace
A quiet path to find your place!

So, get your swift
Not to grim,
Mark your feet
You are a valiant soldier
Turn it around this time,
Crash each barrier.
Because it's been years since you shined,
Yet again you need to shine
Yet again, you have to shine!!!

3. Let them Heal

When the hearts were aching,

The woman turned vocal,

The man turned gentle.

Neither the silence was regal,

Nor the words were lethal.

Let them deal,

Allow them to heal!

In the quiet moments of sorrow,

They will find their tomorrow.

With every word or tear they shed,

Wounds will mend where love is fed!

Yes, life drifted them apart

Yes, they tried very, very hard

Yet the souls couldn't depart.

What now feels like an emotional hazard,

Was that real?

Or just a facade??

What was meant for ages,

Are now burning the bridges.

Devastated they stand

Though, Life goes on!

For healing comes in different forms,

Through whispered peace or raging storms.

Give them space, let time reveal

That every scar can also heal!!!

4. Timeless Muse

On one heavenly night,

The celestials met,

Gazing at the blazing sun,

Beaming with pride

The gentle moon cried,

Oh you, the radiant and the powerful

The Magnanimous, The Golden Globe,

Burning in solitude, all we know!

The source of life,

The source of light

despite your plight.

Look at me,

Nothing is mine,

By your virtue, I shine

Surrounded by gazillions of stars,

Echoing are the tales of my awe

About how mesmerising the night was!

I pity you, determined by destiny

You burn yourself for the sake of humanity

Yet, I am the timeless muse,

Generations will write

All about my beauty!!!

5. The Empty Nest of a Mother

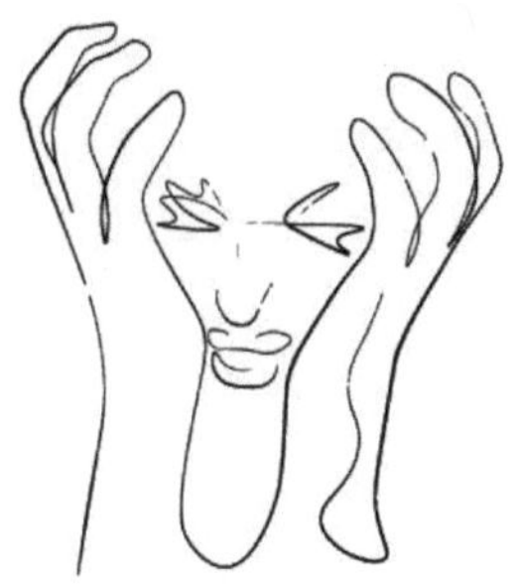

The only treasure to hold,

Not the lustrous silver

Nor the dazzling gold,

It is the love that is beyond measure

The warmest hugs of my mother

Dispelling my fears,

While fighting her own

Embracing my tears,

While concealing her own

Navigating the highs

Persevering through the lows

That remarkable ability

In all circumstances

To love unconditionally

Through all challenges

Without a hint

The resilience she exhibits

When I leave

I do read in her eyes

To build this home

She gave it all; she gave her best

Now, she is left with nothing

Just an EMPTY NEST!

6. The Monsoon!

Don't the monsoons bring back your vivid memory

reflecting on your life in a poignant summary?

The year of strength that you had endured

would be washed off as the torrential rain poured.

It tempts you to get drenched in rain

and your memories thaw

with a sharp excruciating pain

Like a film, you could picture

almost every frame

With the darkest cloud you had ever seen in a while.

but you abandon nature's conspiracy with a counterfeited smile

You look outside through the window pane

You failed to realise,

you are drenched in pain

not in rain.

7. As you grow older

You tend to see beauty all along,
as you grow older,
Beauty in the small fleeting moments
& in moments that seem forever
Beauty in the innocence of the child
& in the wisdom of the wrinkled
Beauty in the shared smile,
& in the genuine connection
Beauty in the lonely tears,
& in the self-companion
Beauty in the wither
& in the blossom

Beauty in the warmth of the Sun
& in the calmness of the moon
Beauty in the awaited
& in the unexpected
Beauty in the new beginnings
Beauty in the things that end
for it Happened!

8. Unconditionally!

In the society we live in
Loving your true self can be hard
While being hard on yourself
becomes the art of coping
Prioritising yourself seems selfish
while the sacrifices seem divine
The pursuit of perfectionism is unrelenting
setting unrealistic standards
leading to self-criticisms
starving of the validations
seeking felicitations
unaware of the fact
You don't need any reason

to love yourself

You just have to be you!

your true self

to love yourself!

unconditionally!!

9. Rendezvous with the Best Version of You!

Be the early-morning coffee

that when mellifluously

runs down the throat

breaks the dawn

emerging sunrise!

Be the first ray of sunshine

that when peeps through the window

promises with glory

a bright new day!

Be the songbird's early call
bringing hope to all
whose melody is honest grace
with a contagious smile on every face!

Be the warmth in every smile you greet
A kindness shared with those you meet
For in the quiet of the morning's start
Lies strength to heal a weary heart

Be the highlighting moment
of the day, when reflected upon
brings a sense of
satisfaction and pride!

Be the reflection of self
that strives to be
through it all
the best version of yourself!

10. The Trajectory of Life

The journey of life is long

with too much at stake

We rise, we fall,

We bend, we break.

Beginnings are soft, with dreams in tow

But in the arc of time, we will fluster and sway

Following the path unseen & unknown

With the choices made, the strength shown

Hold on to it, if we may

Each wave you fight, each crest away

The trajectory of life is a gentle curve

We rise above, we soar, we explore

Every twist and turn we trace

Is etched with fortitude and grace

And in the end,

We will be proud of the line we've drawn

The final race that you just won

Embracing life's new dawn!!!

The journey of life is long.

11. The Silent Fight!

Hey Mama,

I am home and our favourite love story has just begun

I see you wrapping me in lullabies & rhyme

I see your love, so pure, so deep.

but I also see Mama,

A tug on your heart denying you sleep

I hear your silent sobs before the dawn

When the world is hushed

and the shadows long.

I see your exhausted face,

but in your arms, I feel so safe

I see you keep rocking me through the nights

with tender grace.

I see Mama, in the midst of the joys,

your tears fall

I wonder, how you give it all.

12. Secrets of The Soul

Some feelings are best left unsaid,
For the moment they are out,
They lose their very essence,
Fading in the cloud of doubt.

In silence, lies a power deep,
Some feelings, words can't hold,
When it is kept in heart,
It is worth far more than gold.

Lingering in the open air,
No longer they are wrapped in a thought,

What once meant the world,
The meaning is gone, forgot.

Let some words remain unspoken,
The deepest secret to the soul,
For sometimes, what is within,
keeps us whole.

13. Rendezvous with Life's Hardships

When life happens,

It humbles you.

It will strip you away,

The pride that led you astray.

Unlike the easy times,

That flattens you,

With inflated egos & uncalled attitude.

Hard times cultivate,

Humility & gratitude.

The raging storms stimulate,

Resilience & fortitude.

In the face of struggle, wisdom grows.

With every fall, the spirit knows.

In the trials & tribulations, you find your
ground.

A deeper connect, a strength profound.

& When the darker clouds begin to part,

You carry your spark within your heart.

14. Letting Go!

You need to let go,

for your own good!

Few people will refuse to stay,

and few moments will slip away.

It might have once felt right,

but now it's time to release your grip,

Holding on tight is not the victory

Neither losing a part, a sign of defeat.

Letting go would rather,

Help you breathe

Help you grow.

Heal your heart.

With new beginnings

Gather your scattered dreams.

You will see the beauty beyond,

Only when something departs.

15. Comfort in the Absurd

In this long journey of life,

There will be prolonged days

When the world feels out of place.

The promises will be broken

The beliefs will be shaken

Devastating losses,

emotional pain

& what not,

you will have to embrace it all.

But this is not the end of the road.

You will make a new choice

You will learn to cope

Much to your surprise

You will find

Comfort in the Absurd!

16. When my orange could be a pink!

As a kid,

I had my own canvas of colours

& I could paint the world with my own views

My orange could be a pink

and I felt I had my hidden wings

I could count the stars in everyday skies

and see everything with clearer eyes

Every dawn brought something new

Dreams were big, worries a few.

In every shadow, I found a friend
Each day an adventure, without end
The world was a playground, vast and wide
with endless wonders, I couldn't hide

I danced with the breeze and with the rain
Felt no boundaries, only joy, no pain,
With a heart full of hope and mind so free.
The universe belonged to me.
Today, I stand at the expanse of the sea!

17. The Canvas of Life

The beginning of the journey of life,

Is a canvas in shades of white

A field untouched, a surface crisp and bare

Awaiting the touch of your artistic care.

It is the playground for the soul

With your vision, you can control

In the strokes of the brush, moves the wind

colours merge and lines entwine

In its embrace, you will shine.

In every hue, in every smear,

The canvas speaks to those who hear.

It captures moments, rich and stark,

An endless space for every mark.

Let it hold all your stories that were left unsaid,

Let it be the witness to your silent thread.

And when the journey calls for an end

Leave the canvas in the best shades of your life.

18. The true Strength!

Dear Women,

Your strength doesn't lie in the way you look

nor in the way you dress up or that tender smile

but it lies in the courage to be authentic and real.

It doesn't lie in materials or love you earn

But in the wisdom you gather, the lessons you learn.

It doesn't lie in perceiving yourself flawless

But in embracing imperfection with unwavering grace.

It doesn't lie in sacrificing your needs

but in balancing care for others with self-care.

It doesn't lie in enduring in silence

but in your voice,

speaking your truth and making your own choice.

It doesn't lie in being loved by all

but in being true to yourself

even if it means,

Not everyone is happy!

19. Rendezvous with If Only

If only I could see my way

through every night and every day

and attempt to avert the twists of fate

Before it's all too late.

If only I could heal the scars

And stop fighting those inner wars

In the stillness, I would find my peace

Where all my doubts I hope would cease.

If only I could bridge the space

Between the dreams I used to chase
And where I stand, in here and now,
With time, I'd learn just how.

But life is made up of our actions
Not just the wishes or the perceptions
So I'll embrace what is, and yet,
Not live with deep regret.

For 'If Only' is akin to those stars
A longing for the distant Mars.
But in the end, what truly shines,
Is making peace with all life's signs.

If only I could truly see,
That all I need is here in me,
To write the story as it goes
With all its highs and lows.

So I'll let go of 'If Only'

And walk the path that is meant for me,

For in each step, a world awaits,

Beyond the gates of Fate.

20. Someday, Everything Will Make Sense

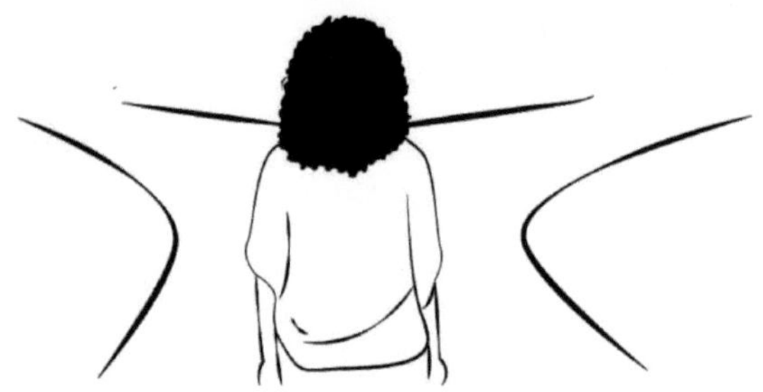

Someday, Everything will make sense
All will fall in place without a pretense
The tangled threads will be smooth and clear
Revealing why we ended up here.

The questions that once plagued the mind
Will fade away, leaving peace behind.
Every tear, every fight, every fear,
Will be seen in a light sincere.

Someday, the puzzle will be complete

And all the pieces will come together
What felt like chaos, just a dance
Guiding us through life's grand expanse.

The struggles that seemed so unfair
Will show their purpose with its share.
The strength they built, the courage gained.
The wisdom earned, the soul sustained.

Someday, we'll look back and smile
At every step, each weary mile
For all the trails that once were grim
Were leading us to where we begin.

Someday, the heart will understand.
The gentle touch of a guiding hand
That every loss and every gain
was part of love's enduring chain.

Someday, everything will make sense,

All will fall in place, immense

And we will see the beauty in scars.

As we reach for the stars.

21. To My Sweet Little One

As you grow, my sweet little one,

Life is a journey, I tell you, a beautiful run

Enjoy the sunshine bright and the skies blue

But you will have to bear dark clouds and the rains too!

There will be moments of joy and delight

When everything seems perfectly right

But, sweetheart, there will be moments, tough and long

Then you'll need to stay brave and strong!

You will meet the kind ones and the unkind too!

But you, my dear, just be you.

For in your heart, there's light so pure,

A guiding star, forever sure!

There'll be hills to climb and streams to cross

But you'll find your way, even when you feel you're lost

With every step you'll learn, you'll grow

Discovering more than you could ever know!

When you stumble or fall and doubts start to creep,

Remember, my love, it's okay to weep.

Know that I am with you in all that you do

Forever and always, my love will guide you!

So, with a heart full of wonder and eyes that gleam

Weave your life with care, as beautiful as your dream

Go, spread your wings and learn to fly

& reach for the highest star,

Remember, my child, I'll be nearby!

Cheering for you, no matter how far.

The world is yours for you to explore

With my love forever more!!!

22. Rendezvous with Serendipity

Serendipity strung its note,

My world changed in a single stroke

A fortuitous encounter, a fleeting glance

Turned life's hustle into a beautiful dance!

Unexpected yet so sweet,

The twist of fate felt so complete.

I found magic in the ordinary

I see my life turning into a beautiful story!

The day we met seemed to be planned.

By those divine hands.

What began as a simple 'Hello'

Grew into love, a bond that would glow!

Though our paths crossed in the most random way

But that moment shaped our everyday

And now every moment feels like a song

leading me right where I belong!

You brought light where shadows fell

In your laughter, I found mine as well

From strangers to partners, hearts intertwined

A gift from the universe, so perfectly timed!

With wonder in every step I take

New paths unfold, no longer opaque

For in that instant, I came to see

The beauty of you and serendipity!

23. Rendezvous with The Light Within

When you trust your journey, come what may

The belief helps you find your way.

For every small leap you take, every path unseen

You will be guided by hands that feel serene.

The winds may howl and eas may roar,

Yet you will be held forevermore.

In moments lost or when you stray

A quiet voice will lead you to stay.

When in doubt, close your eyes and drift within

You will find love and light that lie within.

You will hear a melody that stirs the air,

and fills your heart with a quiet prayer.

The stars above and the earth below

all seem to speak of what they know

and you will hear a gentle whisper calling your name

From realms beyond the earthly frame.

Though life may twist in ways unknown

You will never be truly alone

He will help you find your place

With an endless flow of light and grace.

You will witness the stillness of the soul's retreat

where time and space no longer meet

Awaits a life beyond this death,

in the depths of every breath.

24. Rendezvous with younger self!

In the quiet hush of the evening air,

I wandered back to a place so rare

A forgotten trail where time stood still

Where innocence reigned and dreams could fulfil.

I followed the echoes of laughter pure

The sound of my heart that once was sure

Through fields of wonder, untouched by fear

I walked to the place where my life was dear.

There, beneath the tree of timeless grace

I found her sitting, a familiar face

Wide-eyed and curious, full of glee

She was the innocent version of me.

'Come closer', she said with a beckoning smile,

'Sit with me here, and stay for a while.

You've travelled so far with burdens to bear

But at this moment, there is nothing to fear'.

I sat beside her, unsure at first,

Afraid that the world had done its worst

But as she reached for my hands so small

I felt the weight of the years slowly fall.

We spoke of the days when the sky was wide,

When everything was possible with nothing to hide.

She showed me the dreams I'd locked away

The ones that faded in the harsh light of the day.

'Why did you leave me'? she softly asked,

'Why hide behind the grown-up mask?

I still live in you, though you can't always see,

The part of you that's wild and free'.

Tears welled up as I saw the truth,

The remnants of my forgotten youth.

In the rush of life, I'd let her go,

Buried beneath layers of what I thought I should know...

But now, in this moment, with the sun sinking low,

I realised she was the light in my shadow

The innocence that once knew no bounds

The part of me that still astounds.

We danced through memories, hand in hand
From the backyard swings to castles of sand.
Each step, a reminder of who I used to be,
Before the world taught me to bend and flee.

In her eyes, I found the courage to believe
That magic exists if we're willing to receive
The world can be vast yet simple and kind
If we return to our hearts and clear our minds.

As the night grew deeper, the stars came alive
After ages, I felt the joy of that innocent drive
The curiosity, the wonder, the thrill of it all.
The beauty of moments when we felt so small.

When the rendezvous ended, I opened my eyes,
I looked through the years, through every disguise.
For though we may part in the realm of today,

She will be the part of me that will never stray.

I left that place with a lighter heart,

Knowing that innocence is never too far apart

It lives in the questions, the dreams, the play

In the magic of life, we find along the way.

So now, as I journey with each passing day,

I carry her with me, come what may.

For the rendezvous with my innocent self

Has brought me back to my truest wealth.

25. Rendezvous with self-love!

They say loving someone is beautiful,

No one said, loving myself is not any less.

Why wasn't I aware that my heart was just as worthy

of my own kindness and tenderness?

They preach us to give unconditionally to others

With arms open and wide.

Then why not do the same for my soul??

Why do I hold back and hide?

I have learnt that love is the purest gift.
But never knew how to offer it within.
I never knew how to embrace the flaws,
and how to let self-love begin.

Who said, Loving myself is prideful?
I believe it to be reclaiming my grace
A gentle reminder that I too
Deserve my own embrace.

Loving myself is beautiful
A Promise to be fully met!!

26. Luxury in the struggle

The struggles, as much as you wish to escape

They are the true luxury that gives you an exquisite shape

Sure, the season feels endless and real

Yet, beneath it all, there's more to feel

The burns will fade, but the fire will redefine you

In the ambiguity, clarity will find you

You will discover the luxury of strength and grace

The trials and tribulations will show you the new place.

The place with new seasons, a different space

With unknown skies, new reasons for you to rise

With each struggle and each fight

Find your wings and chase the light!

27. Find your feet

Beyond the noise of others' race,

Where shadows amalgamate and dreams chase,

There lies a space, serene, complete—

A place where you can find your feet.

Comparisons are nothing but traps

That tie your wings and curtail your fly.

They whisper lies, barricading your view

Making you doubt what's real, what's true.

But beyond the mirrors of what they see,

There's a path that's carved for only thee.

With every step, let go of the weight,

Of others' stories, of others' fate.

Find your feet on solid ground,

In the quiet, hear your own sound.

For the journey's yours, not theirs to steer,

And the way becomes clear when you face your fear.

In your stride, you will find your shore

You will see storms crash and victory roar!

Beyond the comparisons, light will greet,

And in that glow, you'll find your feet.

28. The Lone Crusader

When I feel alone in the middle of the night

I see the world has taken its flight,

Here I stand alone, unbowed, unbent,

A lone crusader, my spirit without a dent.

Though it seems there's a lot to bear.

I watch my steps, walk with care

Yet still, I walk this path that is unseen,

It seems to be dark all around, though I feel serene.

Gathering my strength for the endless fight,

I face the darkness with my inner light.

I know I will conquer all my fears

Determined I am, though I can feel my tears.

My heart is full of hope,

Though I do have my moments of doubt.

My heart does beat a little stronger now,

But that's how I am gonna grow!

And though nobody would ever know

The silent wars I am fighting now

A lone crusader I am, standing tall.

Bearing everything, surviving it all!

29. The Reunion!

I met her all over again, finally one afternoon!

A friend that had stayed through the dusk &
dawn.

It took me a while to recognise her,

I thought I had lost the friend in her!

She seemed fragile and faded,

But the stories she carried were endless.

We sat in our favourite corner,

& the sunset cast a golden glow

As the wind rustled through the dusty
window

She uncomfortably fluttered; I held her close.

But the deafening silence filled the space.

She was an invisible barrier between me

and the world outside.

She spoke volumes to my heart without a
sound.

She heard my hidden tales without judgment

Offering me the wisdom and guidance.

With her, it was all magical,

When she started telling her stories,

I was ported to another world

I would roam with her,

Across new lands, far from home.

The air felt cooler,

and the grass softer.

I could feel the warmth beneath my feet,

I could hear the distant murmur in a language
I didn't speak.

Suddenly, the room began to shake

Were the walls crumbling?

My heart raced, I clutched her tightly

and closed my eyes
to escape the impending collapse.
But as I opened them back again
I found myself sitting in the corner,
as if nothing had happened.
Soon the darkness followed,
I couldn't see her,
But she was right there,
Yet I had an unsettling feeling
as if my journey wasn't over.
But I realised she had given me
a glimpse of something deeper.
And though she was my favourite companion
I had to seek life beyond her pages.
I am ready to drift into the dreams
As I hit the hay!
I put her back on the shelf
It is just the beginning!
My favourite book is singing!

30. Unconditional Does exist

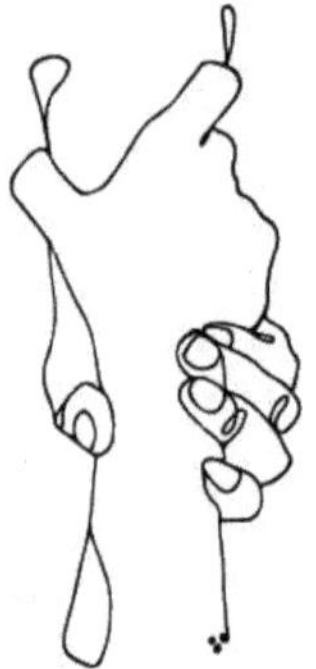

Is there anything unconditional, true,

In a world of give and take, old and new?

Is there any kind of love that holds without demands?

Like that of a parent's heart, like time's sands.

Or like that of the sun that rises without request

Like the season's change at no one's behest

Like the tides that ebb, or the moon's soft glow,

Isn't the river beaming with joy in its steady flow?

Is there a bond that stays through the storm and calms

Like that of a divine prayer or a curing balm?

Doesn't a flower bloom in its gentle ways,

Unconditional, doesn't the nature display?

Is there a friendship that knows no end?

Like that of a destiny, forever meant?

Is there a love shared without a score?

Without a thought of who's less or who's more??

Though life may twist and seasons change,

Will there be someone constant who remains,

Unconditional, pure and kind,

Found only in the heart, the soul, the mind.

Like the light that guides us through the night,

Or that of the flame that burns, forever bright.

Though hard to see and often missed,

Unconditional does exist.

31. Isolated!

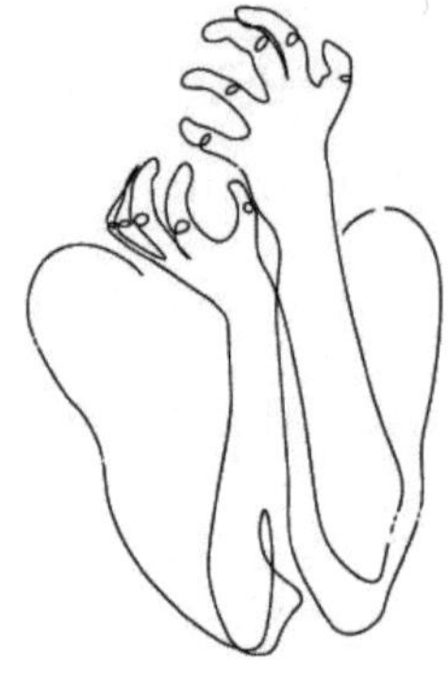

Your experiences are not isolated

Your struggle is not intended

Your path is not any longer,

Your pain is not any stronger

Your solitude is the amplifier

Know that You are not alone

The relief will come

Wait for the turn.

32. The different Road

In your journey of life

You might end up choosing a different road

One not really travelled, not really known.

It might have its own twists and turns,

It might lead you far from your destination.

But you will realise that it holds its own kind of grace,

With every step, you will have something new to embrace

The path will be unknown, but the skies will still be blue,

That road will be beautiful too.

As you move ahead, there lies a view,

A hidden gem meant just for you.

You might not see where it will lead,

But trust in it, and plant your seed.

This journey's yours, and yours alone,

A different road can also feel like home.

Though paths may part but the heart stays true,

And every road holds beauty so new!

33. In the Hustle

In the hustle and the bustle,

You are full of beans,

Chasing every moment,

Living out your dreams.

Yet in all the rushing,

You sometimes miss the boat,

Opportunities drifting by,

Like the destiny, you never wrote.

With energy and passion,

You take on every day,

But in the whirlwind of it all,
Few things are bound to slip away.

So pause within the chaos,
And take a deep breath or two,
For even in the hustle,
There's beauty waiting for you.

34. Burning the midnight fuel

Burning the fuel at midnight,

Yet also the early bird,

You work so hard, chasing dreams,

Driven by every word.

For days like one in a blue moon,

You soar, on cloud nine,

But remember, not too soon,

Mundane days will follow you back again.

So savour each high, embrace each low,

For life is a winding tune,

Through the hustle, let your joy show,
Even on ordinary afternoons.

Hard work bears its shining fruits,
But rest is part of the way,
Celebrate the special days,
And find peace in the grey.

35. The intertwined souls!

My heart holds two souls so dear

One is my soulmate, the other my darling daughter,

One gives me strength, and the other wipes my tears.

Hand in hand, we walk this road without fear

One taught me patience, slow and true

The other is resilience to push through.

When the times are hard, they lift me up,

Always moving, always being and always enough!

One keeps me on my toes all day,

The other helps me in every way!

My little one, with endless cheer,
You fill my world with joy so clear.
And then there's you, my steady guide,
With you, I find peace inside.
Between the two, my world spins bright,
With endless energy and love in sight.
One keeps me grounded, calm and strong,
The other makes every day a song.
With every joy, with every strife
Together, we create this beautiful life!

36. Be the little you!

When you were little and free,

The teacher asked,

'What do you want to be'?

You said you'd be the Prime Minister,

Or the president, standing tall,

Or something even grander,

No dream was too small.

In your naivety, you believed,

The sky was your only limit,

You didn't know it was unachievable,

For your heart had no walls in it.

But then you grew up,
And built your own box,
Shaped by the world,
You joined the flock.

Now, find that *naive* you,
That dreamer within,
Break free of the boundaries,
Let the magic begin.

Rebuild those wild dreams,
Let them take flight,
For within you still lies,
That child of pure light.

37. That's your story!

It is not about the people who believed in you,

Nor those who doubted what you'd do.

It's not about the ones who lied

or those who left you scarred for life.

It is not about their constant gaze,

or the judgements in your darkest days

It is not about the people who stood by you

Nor those who tried to betray.

It is not about the accolades or the fame

Nor those who never spoke your name.

It is not about the crowd or the cheer,

Nor those fleeting moments of fear.

In the end, it is all about you,

Who fought all the battles and made it through

It is your journey, It's about the path you've paved

So when you look back on your way

Remember it, whatever they say

But it is you who defines your truth

It is about you,

You walked through the fire,

Shaped your fate.

That is your story

No one could take.

38. Breaking the mould!

Pretty girls, they say,

Are only made to smile,

Seen but never heard,

Living in denial.

They cast their judgments quickly,

Like shadows on the sun,

Dismissing what's beneath,

Believing beauty means there's none.

But what they fail to see,

Is strength behind the grace,
A mind that's sharp and ready,
With courage to embrace.

And those they call 'mediocre',
Trying to be the smartest,
Are carving out their path,
With every step, the hardest.

For neither beauty nor the plain,
Defines what lies inside,
It's the fire in the heart,
That breaks the mould with pride.

So rise above the labels,
And let your spirit soar,
For no stereotype can hold,
The power at your core.

39. Manifestations!

Why do only the successful speak,
of manifesting dreams?
When it's a truth for everyone,
in all life's diverse streams.
The winners talk about how they dreamed,
and saw it come to light.
But dejected are the ones who failed,
whose ideas were lost from sight.
Yet manifesting isn't just,
the victory at the end,
It is also about the tales of action.
opening doors for new possibilities.

It's in the courage to believe,
through every curve and bend.
For those who fell and lost their way,
Still held a dream inside,
Their stories, though not spoken loud,
Hold lessons that can guide.
Success wears the crown of proof,
But failure has its say,
For in the trying and the hope,
We manifest each day.
So even if the path is hard,
And dreams don't always bloom,
Remember, every step you take,
Creates another room.
Manifestation belongs to all,
Not just the ones who win,
For every dream pursued with heart,
Is where the magic begins.

40. The little humans

Do you see the little humans, with hearts so pure and bright,

They see the world with wonder and treat all things right.

They share their toys and laughter and never see the divide,

Between one friend or another, all stand by each other's side.

Do you see how they forgive without a thought and hug away the pain,

For in their world of innocence, there's no need to explain.

But as the little humans grow, the world begins to change,

They learn of rules and barriers, making it all strange.

The grown-ups speak of limits, who belongs and who does not,

They build up walls with hardened hands; soon, they forget.

They forget the kindness they once had, the humanity they knew,

The simple act of being good and seeing the world anew.

But somewhere deep within, the little human still remains,

Waiting for a moment to break free from the chains.

So let the little humans teach, the grown-ups how to be,

To see the world with open hearts and live with humanity.

41. Let Some Dreams Be Unfulfilled

Let some dreams be unfulfilled,

Not every star is to be caught,

In the silence of the night,

They still shine with every thought.

Let some scars remain unhealed,

For they tell the stories untold,

The battles fought in the quiet,

And the strength that we still hold.

Let some tears gently flow,

Like rivers that find their way,
Through every twist and turn of life,
They cleanse what words can't say.

Let some secrets stay with you,
Hidden deep within your heart,
For not every truth needs sharing,
Some mysteries play their part.

Let some aspirations not be met,
It's okay to not reach the sky,
For in the journey lies the beauty,
In the questions, the reasons why.

So embrace what's left undone,
What's imperfect and yet true,
For every piece of your story,
Is what makes you, you.

42. The Idea of Love!

The Love that begins in the air and feels as light as a breeze,

With picture-perfect moments and effortless ease.

Those stolen glances with the laughter that flies,

In whispered secrets and stars in the skies.

The love is romance oh! so sweet,

With hearts beating fast whenever you meet.

With butterflies in the stomachs and the dreams we create,

The feeling that destiny made us soulmates.

This is the idea of love!

But the love that is found in the work you share,

In the sacrifices made, in the weight that you bear.

It's in the quiet moments when things are tough,

When you stand together, even when it's rough.

The love is changing, growing side by side,

It's facing the challenges, with nothing to hide.

It's choosing each other again and again,

Building a life through joy and pain.

This is love.

43. What is life!

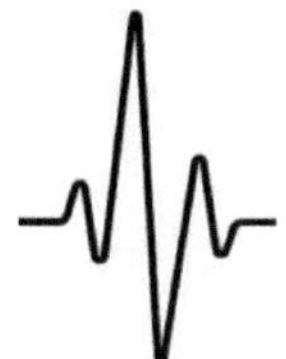

What is this life but fleeting dust,
With few moments of assurance
But then the broken trust?
We chase the sun, we seek the light,
Without realising that everything eventually
Dissolves in an endless night!

We build our walls, we write our names,
Few years from now, it won't be the same
The stars will burn, the earth will fade,
And all our dreams will be unmade.

We make the castles tall
Which are meant to fall

Meaning crumbles, purpose breaks,
In the void, all hope forsakes.
We wander through this hollow space,
And find no mercy, no embrace.

For nothing waits beyond the dark,
No whispered truth, no hidden spark.
Just endless silence, cold and bare,
A universe that does not care.

44. The Irony of now!

The irony is that we live in the present,

Yet our minds keep wandering far and wide,

We neither stop lingering in the echoes of the past,

Nor cease longing for what the future might hide.

We stand in the moment but never want to stay,

We keep chasing shadows of what's been,

Or dreaming of a distant day,

Where we hope our lives might begin.

The present keeps calling, but we seldom hear,

Its whispers, drowned by time,

We keep grasping at what's no longer near,

Or reaching for mountains yet to climb.

But here we are, in the fleeting now,

The only place that's real,

Yet torn between what was, what will be,

We forget to simply feel.

Why don't we let the past rest where it lies,

And let the future wait for its turn,

Let us realise that the present is where life truly thrives,

And let all our worries burn.

45. My Dream Home!

Someday, I wish to build my dream home!

A home far from this human race

A home may be in the mountains high,

Where I can sing with the winds my favourite lullabies.

Where my bathing tub is, the river is so clear,

Its cool waters washing away all my fears.

I will fly on the wings of birds,

And gauging the skies, unbound by words.

I will dance with the clouds in my own way,

And greet the dawn with each new day.

I’ll make my meals with the nectar,
And will bloom like a flower!
I will see places that only books have shown,
Unfold my dreams and uncover mysteries!

In the mountains, I’ll find my soul’s retreat,
With rivers to bathe in and the earth beneath.
I will begin my day with the sun,
And in nature’s grasp, I'll find my home.

46. To the ones that love the most!

Sometimes we hold resentment close,
Against those who love us the most.
Not out of hatred or disdain,
But unknowingly, they aggravate the pain.

They've always wanted the best for you,
But their words can sting, cut through.
Their gentle nudges, though they care,
Can feel like burdens hard to bear.

Yet it's they who see our deepest flaws,
And offer truth without applause.
They call out wrongs you'd rather hide,
With love that stands strong, side by side.

It's hard to see through wounded eyes,
That their advice is your greatest prize.
Forgive them for their harsh critique,
For it's love that makes their voice so meek.

In time, you'll see what they have done,
Was not to hurt but guide you, one by one.
So hold them close and let it be known,
They're the ones who've helped you grow.

Forgive them, for they love you the most,
And in their care, you are never lost.

47. The Sorry

Sorry, the briefest word carrying
greatest relief.
It can mend the cracks
and heal the seams!
In moments of pride,
It is hard to say
But it will for sure
soften the heart
once cold and closed,
And bring back warmth
where love once froze.

And no!

It's not a sign of weakness

As many perceive,

Instead, the strength

to bear the humble cross.

It helps retain

what matters most,

Keeps us close

Ensuring nothing is lost.

A bridge to span

the deepest rift,

A simple word

a priceless gift.

So let it flow

with grace and ease,

For in 'sorry',

we find our peace.

It's a small word

with a mighty start,

That helps to heal

a wounded heart.

48. What if?

How would it be if we could start anew,
With a clean slate, fresh as morning dew?
Wouldn't we choose things differently
This time with a clearer mind
And leaving everything behind!
What if we could lose it all,
Every burden, big or small?
The weight that drags our spirits low,
Released in winds, allowed to go.
How would it be to circle in time,
And return to days that felt sublime?
To find the joy we once embraced,
Before the years had left their trace.
How would it be to relive the only beautiful past,
Hold onto moments we wish would last?

To mend what's broken, heal what's torn,
And find again what was once worn.
But time moves forward, never still,
Yet dreams of return linger at will.
Perhaps it's not the past we seek,
But a chance to grow, to rise, not weak.
For in every loss, there's space to gain,
To turn the hurt into something sane.
And though we cannot go back in time,
We can still create new days that shine.

49. The Strange Connect!

I saw a girl from my terrace,
As I sipped my coffee warm.
She walked with quiet grace,
Yet carried a different charm.

Her clothes were worn and simple,
A sign of humble days.
But something about her presence
Held me in a gentle gaze.

She moved with purpose, steady,
Unaware of eyes that trailed,
And in her steps, I sensed
A story yet unveiled.

Though life had marked her with its hand,
There was light within her eyes.
I followed her until she slipped
Beyond the morning skies.

A fleeting moment, brief yet deep,
A stranger passing by.
She left me with a quiet thought
That lingers in my mind.

50. Daughters are Precious!

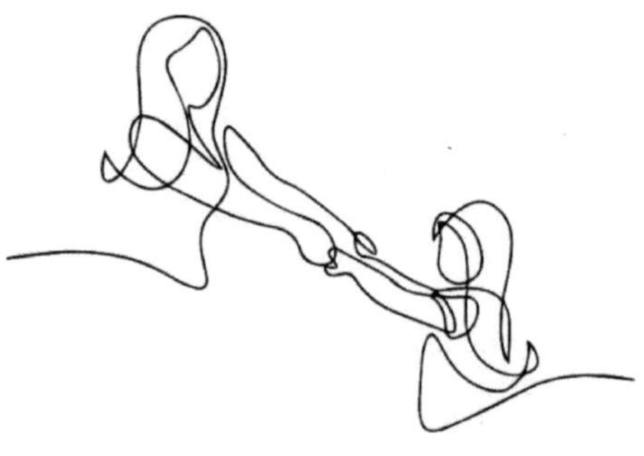

When she was two, with words so few,

She looked at me with eyes so true.

In her innocent voice, she softly said,

'You're my best friend', as she laid her head.

She didn't know much, yet her heart was clear,

She'd always love me, year after year.

In moments when I felt so low,

Her tiny words made my spirit glow.

At three, she brought me tablets with care,
As if her small hands could ease every despair.
She helped with chores, her heart so pure,
A little soul, so willing to endure.

At four, when she first saw me on stage
her pride would shine,
As if the world were hers and mine.
How proud she was, and how proud was I,
Together, we reached for the sky.

These moments, though simple, will forever remain,
In the chambers of my heart, like a soft refrain.

51. Change is must!

It's not easy to change,

but we must,

To evolve from the ashes,

to rise from the dust.

Clinging to the old

for the sake of pride

Is a folly that keeps

the soul locked inside.

Refusing to grow,

just to remain the same,

Is to stagnate

in the comfort of your own name.

For the world turns,

and seasons shift,

And life demands we, too, uplift.

Don't say, 'I will not change, not ever',

For that is to shun the road to endeavour.

If the path leads to something better,

Why resist, why bind yourself to the tether?

To change is to learn, to transform, to renew,

To shed the skin that no longer fits you.

So embrace the discomfort, the unknown ahead,

For in that journey, true life is fed.

Stubbornness for its own sake is foolish, you'll see,

But growth—that's where freedom will always be.

52. The Curse

A good memory is a burdensome curse,
An intricate web, intricately diverse.
It clings like ivy to the walls of thought,
Imprinting moments better left unsought.

You remember the details, fine and precise,
Each thread of joy entwined with sacrifice.
What once was bliss now lingers too long,
A haunting echo, a melancholic song.

To hold onto the past is a grievous weight,

Yet the mind insists on opening the gate.

The heart, a prisoner to times once kind,

Struggles to release what binds the mind.

To let go, they say, is the path to peace,

But memories resist—they rarely cease.

They flood the soul, uninvited, relentless,

Turning contentment into something defenceless.

For happiness demands a certain release,

A gentle forgetting to find inner peace.

Yet the mind, so cruel, clutches tight,

And in that grip, we lose the light.

So, a good memory becomes our bane,

A reminder of joy, now shadowed in pain.

And to let go is a task so steep,

Yet necessary for a heart to sleep.

53. The night of solitude

In love with the night of solitude, I dwell,

Wrapped in shadows where quiet truths swell.

The darkness speaks in whispers, arcane and deep,

A silent sanctuary where my thoughts can creep.

My songs, unspoken, take flight in the void,

Echoing off stars in melodies deployed.

They rise and fall with the rhythm of dreams,

Unseen by the day's relentless beams.

The vision in my mind, an elusive art,

Paints worlds untouched by the waking heart.

In this abyss, I craft my realm,

A place where reason loosens its helm.

Here, I wander through ethereal haze,
Each step untethered by time's cruel maze.
The night becomes both my muse and guide,
Where my inner self dares to reside.

This solitude is no desolate space,
But a refuge where I meet my own grace.
In the quiet hum of the night's embrace,
I find my truth, a mirrored face.

Yet the world, in daylight's glare,
Cannot fathom the depths I wear.
So I retreat, beneath the moon's pale hue,
Where only shadows know what's true.

54. Each one is unique!

Each one is unique,

a path of their own,

A journey to travel,

a seed to be sown.

In time, we all find

what we're destined to see,

For each soul holds

its own mystery.

Everyone stumbles,

but learns to rise,

Finding their way

beneath changing skies.

Through winding roads

and twists of fate,

We each find our rhythm,

sooner or late.

Don't be scared

where you stand,

If you are here,

you'll soon understand

This moment is just a passing view,

And trust, in time, you'll make it through.

The road may be tough, the night may be long,

But strength is found in the heart's quiet song.

So keep walking forward, with courage anew,

For everyone here has the power to breakthrough.

55. The Waiting

When waiting is tough,
and time feels slow,
The hours refuse to let you go,
When each second drags with heavy weight,
And patience wears thin beneath the wait!

Make the waiting sweet,
embrace the pause,
Let go of the need to rush the cause.
For time, though stubborn, has its flow,
Unfolding secrets we don't yet know.

Instead of yearning to accelerate,
Count the moments—don't berate.
Each tick of the clock, a note in a song,
A rhythm that carries you along.

Savour every beat

Only then, life is complete!

56. Tug of War

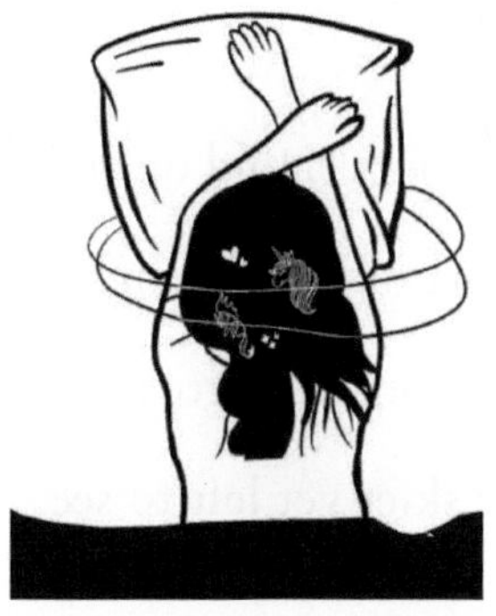

A tug of war between my heart and mind.

Reminding me of the times insane

Guarding me against the potential pain

My mind clings to what it knows,

The heart yearns where hope flows.

I have desires

But then there are doubts too,

A tangled thread,

Each thought is a battle in the head.

The poor heart is caught in between,
Wishing to stay yet longing to dream.

One side whispers, 'Hold on tight',
To the comfort of familiar light.
The other beckons, 'Let go, be free',
For there are skies yet left to see.

In this struggle, the heart must choose,
Which pull to follow, which path to lose.
Yet perhaps, in the tension's sway,
Both sides have something true to say.

For in every tug and gentle strain,
There's wisdom hidden in the pain.
A balance is found when the truth is near.
In the tug of war, the lesson is clear.

57. Life is like Legos!

Life is like Legos,
piece by piece,
Built with care,
but never at ease.
No matter how hard
you try to hold,
Sometimes it falls,
sometimes it folds.
It crumbles down,
despite your plans,
Slips through your fingers,
out of your hands.
But don't despair,
don't let tears flow,
For Legos can be rebuilt,
as you know.

Gather the pieces,
start once more,
Each time you rebuild,
you're stronger than before.
With patience and courage,
you'll create anew,
A structure more resilient,
a vision more true.
So when life tumbles,
don't just cry,
Pick up the pieces,
and aim for the sky.
For every fall
is just a chance,
To rebuild your dreams,
to give life another dance.

58. When reality is better than Dream!

I have a life

Where reality is better than my dreams,

I found myself in life's brightest beams.

The world is more vivid than my mind could weave,

Offering moments that I almost can't believe.

Dreams, once cherished in slumber's soft glow,

Seem pale compared to what life can bestow.

The touch of the wind, the warmth of the sun,

The joy of my journey just begun.

In these moments, I see so clear,

That reality holds its own magic here.

It's more than fantasy could ever create,

A wondrous blend of love and fate.

59. Mistakes don't define you!

Mistakes are not forever,
they don't define who you are
or who you could be!
It’s a moment in time
where your stars didn’t align.
Rise above it
let go of the weight,
Through every fall
There’s a chance to create.
The past may linger,
but it’s certainly not your fate,
In your hands lies a future,
Just like a clean slate.
You are more than
the errors of yesterday,

You can shape a new life
in your own way.
With each misstep,
A lesson unfolds,
In the broken pieces,
a story told.
But don't dwell in the echoes
of what went wrong,
For within you,
the strength to move on is strong.
Rise above it,
lift your gaze,
Towards brighter tomorrows,
uncharted days.
Mistakes aren't chains
they're steps in disguise,
Leading you onwards to where hope lies.
So take that chance,
rebuild anew,

Make a life that's more than

what you knew.

For mistakes aren't forever

they're just a part

Of the journey that shapes

your resilient heart.

60. The Usual today is Tomorrow!

Don't waste your days in waiting for tomorrow,

It's not a place where dreams erase sorrow.

Tomorrow is no distant, perfect land,

It's as usual as today, as plain, as planned.

Why wait for the magic of a far-off day,

When right here, right now, there's so much to say?

Why not make this moment grand and bold,

In the warmth of now, where life unfolds?

Tomorrow comes with its own set of cares,

Not a fairy tale that suddenly repairs.

So, grasp today with both hands tight,

And turn this ordinary into something bright.

For life is here, not in a distant year,

And what you seek is already near.

Make this day grand, don't wait for the chance,

Create your joy, take your stance.

61. Learn but with a Purpose!

It's indeed great to learn

& let your mind expand,

But here you need to understand

Learn with a purpose,

with a goal in hand.

For random knowledge,

It's vast and wide,

Won't fulfil the yearning

that burns inside.

You can gather facts,

let your mind explore,

But without direction

you'll crave something more.

A sea of wisdom

may flood your way,

Yet without focus,

you'll drift astray.

To learn with intent is

to chart your course,

To follow the path

with deliberate force.

Each lesson a step,

each fact a guide,

Moving you closer

to what's inside.

So learn with purpose,

let your goals align,

With the knowledge

that helps your dreams to shine.

For in that focus,

you'll find your way,

And turn your learning into something

That stays!

62. The New Story

As you are all set to build a new story,

Choose your characters with deliberate glory.

Remember the missteps from tales of old,

Why the beauty faded, why dreams turned cold.

This time, be cautious, be wise and clear,

Let each choice reflect what you hold dear.

You are the author, the pen's in your hand,

Shape your world, design your land.

Be the hero who rises through the fight,

Let your enemies push you towards the light.

Their presence, a force that sharpens your will,

A reason to climb each daunting hill.
Craft a story that speaks to your soul,
Let it be rich; let it be whole.
For this time, you'll write with a deeper grace,
A tale that time itself can't erase.
Let this be one of the best you've known,
A narrative where you fully own
Every twist, every turn, every page you pen,
Creating a journey worth living again.

63. He Knows!

No one,

No one sees the battles you fight,

Your moments of doubt,

Your search for the light.

But why care ??

Your God does!

Only He knows the weight you bear,

The whispered hopes,

The earnest prayer

He's seen the path you trod

The truth hidden from the world

It is between you and your God!

It's not for others to understand and what lies ahead.

So walk your path with courage and grace,

Knowing that your journey is held in his embrace.

It is between you and your God alone,

A bond that is yours, a faith you've grown

The way you reach for his guiding hand.

For faith is personal, a sacred thread,

Woven between the hearts.

64. The Power of Ageing!

I never knew that ageing could be so powerful,

You shed all the insecurities

That once seemed bountiful

Finally, the goals are clear

And the vision is defined

No longer you are held back

With fears in mind

Unscared, unshaken

Realising the power within

You know the beauty

Of the traces on the face

And each story that lies

In the wrinkles

Those eyes have seen so much

Seeking no validation

No articulation

Whatsoever!

Holding memories of autumn and spring

There is yet so much to live through the joy
and the pain!

65. The Invaluable!

We value so much
of the valuable things,
But often we overlook
what's priceless!
We chase what glitters,
since it is hard to obtain
But forget the rain
that washes away pain.
The laughter of a friend,
the warmth of a smile,
The peaceful moments

that make life worthwhile.
These invaluable things
seem free to the eye,
So easily ignored as time slips by.
But they're not free
we must choose them with care,
For they're the treasures
beyond compare.
When they're gone,
we suddenly see,
We'd give up the world
for what used to be.
The gentle touch,
the loving embrace,
The everyday beauty
we can't replace.
It's the simpler, invaluable things
we should treasure,
They are the heartbeat,

the soul of life,
Beyond the noise,
beyond the strife.
So pause and choose
what truly matters,
Before the chance
to cherish scatters.
Hold on to the moments,
the love, the grace,
For they are the riches
time can't erase.

66. Time only moves Forward!

Missing someone is fine,

But never wish for the reversal of time.

As time is meant to move forward,

Then why do you wish to stay?

The ache you feel is part of the love,

A reminder of the bond!

The pain might seem endless

But time with its own mysterious ways

Will soothe it; just care a little less!

You will be okay, that is for sure,

Though the longing feels too deep to endure.

Time has a way of making things right,

Turning the darkness back into light.

There is beauty in the space they leave,

In the echoes of laughter, in the memories you weave.

For though they are gone, their essence remains,

In the quiet moments, in the soft refrains.

It's in the scent of the morning air,

In the way, the sunlight touches your hair.

It's in the songs that make your heart swell,

In every story, you long to tell.

Hold on to the love that still endures,

Through the changing seasons, it reassures.

Missing them is part of the path you tread,

But life continues, with hope ahead.

Let the absence be not just a void,

But a place where beauty is employed.

For love transcends the bounds of time,

And in its absence, you still find the rhyme.

Though they are gone, their light shines on,

In every dusk, in every dawn.

You carry them with you, wherever you go,

In the dance of life, in the gentle flow.

67. Let your Emotions talk!

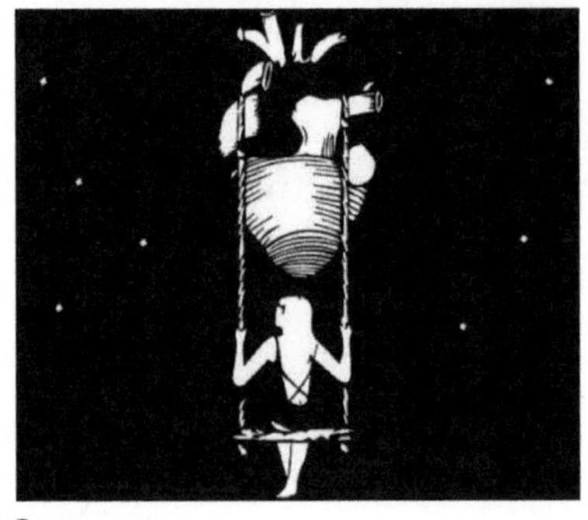

Laugh often,

let joy fill your days,

In moments small,

in countless ways.

Cry often, too,

for tears are real,

A release for the heart,

a way to feel.

Let your emotions flow,

wild and free,

Don't hold them back

they're part of thee.
For bottled feelings
weigh you down,
But open hearts
wear no frown.
You are gold,
pure and bright,
Shining with your own
inner light.
Let it go in your
own spree,
Live life
with all its honesty.
The highs, the lows
the in-between,
Every emotion,
every dream.
You are precious,
just as you are!

68. Untie your Wings!

Why did you tie your wings,

And when did you ground yourself to earthly things?

I know you wished to soar high,

To fathom the vast and open sky.

Why did you freeze your feet in place?

And when did you let the world confine your space?

I know you were born to migrate all across, to roam,

To find your path, to call it home.

Did doubt whisper in your ear?
Sowing the clouds of doubt and weaving fear?
Or did the weight of the world below,
Convince you not to let go?

Untie your wings, let them spread wide,
Feel the wind, let it be your guide.
Melt the ice beneath your toes,
Step into the journey that only you know.

Freedom waits beyond the fear,
A brighter world, crystal clear.
So why stay bound when you can be free?
Release yourself, embrace the sea.

You were made to fly, to feel the breeze,
To drift along with ease and peace.
So don't hold back, don't freeze your heart,
Let yourself bloom; let yourself restart.

69. Someone Having Your Back!

Someone having your back is a gift so rare,

A steadfast presence in times of despair.

In the turbulence of life's unpredictable sea,

They are the anchor, the constant you need to be free.

It's the quiet assurance in their gentle touch,

The knowing glance that says so much.

They stand with you when the world feels cold,

Offering warmth and a hand to hold.

When you stumble and falter on your way,

Their support is a light that brightens the grey.

They lift you up when you feel weak,

And cheer you on when you dare to speak.

Their faith in you is a beacon bright,

Guiding you through the darkest night.

In their presence, you find a haven of peace,

A safe retreat where anxieties cease.

They offer strength when yours is spent,

A source of comfort, a heart so bent.

Through the highs and lows, they remain steadfast,

A reminder that true bonds are meant to last.

Their belief in you is a silent, enduring grace,

A mirror reflecting your courage in their face.

They are the gentle push when you need to strive,

The reason you find the will to thrive.

In moments of joy, they share your delight,

In times of sorrow, they hold you tight.

Their loyalty is a song that never fades,

A melody of love through life's charades.

So cherish those who walk beside you,

Who see you through, who stand true.

For someone having your back is a rare, precious bond,

A testament to the love and trust that responds.

Their support is the strength that makes you whole,

A guiding light for your heart and soul.

In every challenge, their presence you find,

A testament to the enduring ties that bind.

70. Go, Where You Belong!

When you feel that you don't belong to a certain place,

It might be strange or a familiar sight.

An alien or a friendly face

Don't stay for long, not overnight.

The more you linger, the more you will see,

That this place was never meant to be.

It doesn't mean you are the flaw,

Just that life's pushing you to heed its law.

You are not the problem, don't doubt your soul,

You've simply outgrown your role.

For everyone has a place to call their own,

A space where seeds of truth are sown.

So, when you feel the tug to leave,

Listen close, it's time to believe.

There's a new horizon just for you,

A world waiting bright and true.

Know that you belong somewhere more,

Where your spirit will soar and hearts adore.

Because the ones that fit here might not fit there,

That's life's dance, its constant flair

There is a place for everyone,

And in that space, your true life has begun.

71. To All Fathers

To all fathers,

You are the heart of our home.

We know your nights are sleepless and the days endless,

Yet you keep giving your all in ways that are countless.

The quiet strength that you have always shown

Smiling through sacrifices, love is grown.

In the tapestry of life, you are the strongest thread.

A steady hand always guiding, without words being said.

Weaving the wisdom through the windy days,
In every challenge and doubt we face.
Your patience is deep and love is profound,
Lifting us up when we are down.
You are that guiding star,
whose light would never fade.
So, here's to you,
With gratitude bright.
Even when you are out of sight,
Your love is a treasure
A bond that won't sever.

72. The Architect

Have you ever paused to wonder,
Who governs your highs and the lows?
Who guides how your journey flows?
Is there any chart of fate that owes?
Or the stars that align??
Perhaps destiny's grand design?
That keeps it all just fine.
Who decides your rise and fall??
Is it your strength that keeps you tall?
Or is it just a mix of chance and will?
Is it about the opportunities you greet?
Is it you, the company you keep?
Of all the people that you meet?
Your friends or the foes.
Is it your choices?
Your Yes and the No's

Or is it simply what you love?

Maybe it has got nothing to do

With what is happening above.

9 789363 301863

Printed by Libri Plureos GmbH in Hamburg,
Germany